# Delicious Mea Jars

*50 Delicious Meals in Mason Jars Recipes For Breakfast, Lunches, Snacks, Or Dinner That Are Simple And Easy To Prepare, And Incredibly Mouthwatering!*

**Sarah Brooks**

Copyright © 2015 Sarah Brooks

## STOP!!! Before you read any further....Would you like to know the secrets of Anti-Aging?

If your answer is yes, then you are not alone. Thousands of people are looking for the secret to reducing wrinkles, looking younger, and maintaining a youthful appearance.

If you have been searching for these answers without much luck, you are in the right place!

Not only will you gain incredible insight in this book, but because I want to make sure to give you as much value as possible, right now for a limited time you can get full **100% FREE access to a VIP bonus EBook** entitled **Anti-Aging Made Easy!**

### Just Go Here For Free Instant Access: www.LuxyLifeNaturals.com

## Legal Notice

All rights reserved. Without limiting the rights under the copyright reserved above, no part of this publication may be reproduced, stored in or introduced into a retrieval system, or transmitted, in any form, or by any means (electronic, mechanical, photocopying, recording, or otherwise) without the prior written permission of the copyright owner and publisher of this book. This book is copyright protected. This is for your personal use only. You cannot amend, distribute, sell, use, quote or paraphrase any part or the content within this eBook without the consent of the author or copyright owner. Legal action will be pursued if this is breached.

## Disclaimer Notice

Please note the information contained within this document is for educational and entertainment purposes only. Considerable energy and every attempt has been made to provide the most up to date, accurate, relative, reliable, and complete information, but the reader is strongly encouraged to seek professional advice prior to using any of this information contained in this book. The reader understands they are reading and using this information contained herein at their own risk, and in no way will the author, publisher, or any affiliates be held responsible for any damages whatsoever. No warranties of any kind are expressed or implied. Readers acknowledge that the author is not engaging in the rendering of legal, financial, medical, or any other professional advice. By reading this document, the reader agrees that under no circumstances is the author, publisher, or anyone else affiliated with the production, distribution, sale, or any other element of this book responsible for any losses, direct or indirect, which are incurred as a result of the use of information contained within this document, including, but not limited to, errors, omissions, or inaccuracies. Because of the rate with which conditions change, the author and publisher reserve the right to alter and update the information contained herein on the new conditions whenever they see applicable.

## Table Of Contents

Introduction

Chapter 1 - Why Mason Jar Meals?

Chapter 2 - Breakfast Jar Recipes

Chapter 3 - Lunch Jar Recipes

Chapter 4 - Dinner Jar Recipes

Chapter 5 - Snack Jar Recipes

Chapter 6 - Dessert Jar Recipes

Chapter 7 - Salad Jar Recipes

Chapter 8 - Using Mason Jar Meals To Lose Weight

Chapter 9 - Planning For Make Ahead Mason Jar Meals

Chapter 10 - Storage Tips And Foods To Avoid When Making Mason Jar Meals

Conclusion

Preview Of: "DIY Household Hacks: Ultimate DIY Household Hacks Guide! Save Time, Money And Effort, Increase Productivity And Get Stuff Done With 120 Proven And Smart Household Hacks to Make Life Easier!"

Free Bonus Offer!

# Introduction

I want to thank you and congratulate you for purchasing the book, "Delicious Meals in Mason Jars: 50 Delicious Meals in Mason Jars Recipes For Breakfast, Lunches, Snacks, Or Dinner That Are Simple And Easy To Prepare, And Incredibly Mouthwatering!"

This "Delicious Meals In Mason Jars" book contains all the information you need to get started on the art of mason jar meals. From planning make ahead meals to proper storage for your meals, you've learn everything you need to know about preparing mason jar meals.

This book is also packed with easy to make and downright affordable recipes that you can make in the comforts of your own home. You don't have to be chef to whip up delicious meals. With this guide, you can impress your family and friends with tried and tested recipes that are guaranteed to be crowd pleasers.

Thanks again for purchasing this book, I hope you enjoy it!

# Chapter 1 - Why Mason Jar Meals?

I started noticing mason jar meals early last year when I was on the scouring online for easy to make lunch ideas. A lot of moms were raving online how fresh and easy to make mason jar salads were. I decided to give it a try myself and after a year of trial and error, here I am. Writing a book on how you can make your very own mason jar meals at home.

But what's the big deal about mason jar meals anyway?

Aside from the fact that they're quite kitschy, mason jars keep salads fresh or much longer. You just get a better seal with the lid compared to plastic containers.

Another thing that I love is that you can properly portion your food with mason jars. I have the tendency to overeat but now, I'm able to eat the right portion with the help of the jars.

Also, I can eat my meals straight from the jar, especially on days when I find myself too busy to prepare a proper meal. I just pop a jar open and start eating. When I'm done, I pop the jar in the dishwasher, and voila! I don't have to worry about cleanup.

There are a lot more benefits to mason jar meals. With a bit of creativity, you'll be creating your own signature mason meal recipes in no time.

I hope you enjoy the journey as much as I did.

# Chapter 2 - Breakfast Jar Recipes

### *Simple Eggs*

Ingredients:

- 4 large eggs
- 4 slices of bacon, cut into chunks
- 1 small green onions, minced
- 1 cup button mushrooms, thinly sliced
- 1 teaspoon flour
- 1 tablespoon butter
- 1 tablespoon chives, minced
- ¼ cup of chicken stock
- Salt and pepper

Preparation:

Cook bacon until brown.

Add the mushrooms and the green onions and cook for 3 minutes.

Add the flour and the chicken stock and bring to a boil.

Prepare 4 glass jars and rub some butter on the bottom and inside edges. Pour some of the bacon and mushroom mixture evenly in each jar and break one egg on top.

Season with salt and black pepper to taste.

Place the 4 jars into a big cooking pot add water until it reaches the middle of your jars. Bring to a medium-high heat and cook until the eggs set.

Sprinkle s chives on top before serving.

### *Bacon and Eggs*

Ingredients:

- 4 eggs
- 4 slices turkey bacon
- 1 handful fresh spinach
- 1/4 cup shredded cheese
- Salt and pepper

Preparation:

Mix eggs, cheese, and spinach in a bowl. Season with salt and pepper to taste.

Pour mixture into a mason jar.

Microwave for up 90 seconds, checking often.

Cook bacon slices until crisp then crumble on top of egg

## *Blueberry Cheesecake Granola*

Ingredients:

- Blueberries
- Granola
- Almonds, crushed
- Greek yogurt
- Cream cheese

Preparation:

Whip cream cheese, Greek yogurt and almonds in a bowl.

Add a layer of granola in the mason jar then add the yogurt mixture.

Add fresh blueberries, add another dollop of the yogurt mixture, then top with more granola.

## *Spiced Overnight Oats*

Ingredients:

- 1/4 cup steel cut oats
- 1/2 cup milk
- Dash of spice (Cinnamon, nutmeg and ginger)
- Sugar

Preparation:

Mix the first 3 ingredients in a bowl and then pour into a mason jar.

Cover with lid and let the jar to sit in the refrigerator overnight.

Microwave for 1 minute to before serving. Or you can eat it cold if you prefer.

Add sugar according to taste.

## *Honey Cinnamon Morning*

Ingredients:

- ¼ cup granola
- ½ cup Greek Yogurt
- 1 tablespoon Flax or Chia Seeds
- 1 teaspoon Honey
- Dash of cinnamon

Preparation:

Mix together yogurt, flax or chia seeds, honey and cinnamon in a bowl.

Layer granola and yogurt mixture in a jar.

Chill in refrigerator for a couple of hours before serving.

## *Nutella Oats*

Ingredients:

- 1/4 cup cut steel cut oats
- 1 tablespoon Nutella
- 1/2 cup Milk
- Fresh strawberries
- Yogurt (optional)

Preparation:

Combine oatmeal, Nutella and milk in a bowl. Mix ingredients until smooth.

Top with strawberries and leave in the refrigerator overnight.

Top off with a dollop of yogurt and strawberries before serving.


## *Pumpkin Crunch*

Ingredients:

- 1/4 cup granola
- 1/2 cup yogurt with a drop of vanilla essence
- 1 tablespoon pumpkin pie filling
- Dash of cinnamon, nutmeg and ginger

Preparation:

Mix pumpkin, yogurt and spices in a bowl.

Layer granola & yogurt mixture in mason jar.

Chill overnight before serving.


## *Quinoa and Fruit*

Ingredients:

- 1/2 cup quinoa
- 1/4 cup milk
- 1/4 cup cream
- 1/2 cup Water
- Fresh strawberries
- Banana
- Almonds
- Honey

Preparation:

Rinse & drain quinoa.

Bring milk, water, and cream to a boil. Add quinoa and bring to a boil again.

Let it simmer for 12 minutes.

Fluff quinoa with fork after letting it cool down for 5 minutes.

Layer quinoa, almonds and fruits into a jar.

Serve warm with a drizzle of honey on top.

## *French Toast in a Jar*

Ingredients:

- 1/3 loaf of bread, cubed
- 1 1/2 cup milk
- 2 eggs, beaten
- 2 tablespoon melted butter
- 1 tablespoon vanilla essence
- 1/4 cup sugar
- 1 tablespoon cinnamon
- Blueberries
- 1/4 cup maple syrup

Preparation:

Put a layer of cubed bread in the jars.

Combine milk, Eggs, butter, vanilla, sugar, cinnamon, and blueberries in a separate bowl.

Pour mixture evenly into jars.

Cover jars and store upside down in fridge overnight.

Heat oven to 375 and cook uncovered jars until top is golden brown.

Let cool and top with maple syrup before serving.

# Chapter 3 - Lunch Jar Recipes

## *Baked Potatoes*

Ingredients:

- 1 packet instant mashed potato flakes
- 1 cup milk
- ½ cup Sour cream
- ½ cup Shredded cheese
- 2 sprigs green onion, chopped
- Bacon bits, cooked
- Salt and Pepper

Preparation:

Cook instant mashed potatoes according to the instructions.

Stir cheese, sour cream, bacon into the mashed potatoes. Season with salt and pepper to taste.

Spoon the mixture into mason jars and top with more cheese and bacon.

Bake at 350F until the cheese melts.

Garnish with chopped green onions before serving.

## *Chicken Cordon Bleu*

Ingredients:

- 6 Chicken breast cutlets, cooked
- 6 slices smoked ham, cooked
- 6 slices Swiss cheese
- 1/2 cup melted butter
- 1 1/2 cup Plain Panko bread crumbs
- 1 teaspoon dried parsley
- Salt and pepper

Preparation:

Roll chicken, ham, and cheese together into a log shape.

Cut into even slices that will fit your mason jars.

Place each spiral into a wide-mouth mason jar.

Mix melted butter, parsley flakes, and Panko Bread Crumbs. Season with salt and pepper to taste.

Divide the crumbs evenly over jars.

Bake jars at 375F until crumbs turn golden.

Remove from oven and cool completely before serving.

## **Corn Dogs**

Ingredients:

- 6 hot dogs, cooked, cut in half
- 3 cups yellow corn meal mix, self-rising
- 6 eggs
- 1/2 cup sour cream
- 1 1/2 cups milk
- 1/4 cup oil
- 3/4 cup sugar

Preparation:

mix all of the ingredients together except for hot dogs.

Pour mix into mason jars, leaving half an inch at the top.

Place the hot dogs in the middle of the batter.

Bake until corn bread is cooked through and golden.

Cool completely before serving.

Serve with a side of mustard.

### Easy Lasagna

Ingredients:

- ½ packet wide egg noodles, cooked
- 1 egg
- 3 cups marinara sauce
- 3 cups ricotta cheese
- 1 cup parmesan cheese
- 2 cups mozzarella cheese
- Salt and pepper

Preparation:

Mix noodles with 2 cups of sauce.

In a bowl mix together egg, ricotta, parmesan cheese, and mozzarella.

Fold cheese mixture gently in with the noodles.

Place in jars and top with remaining sauce.

Top with Parmesan cheese.

Bake at 350F until top browns.

Allow to cool completely before serving.

### Easy Peasy Pasta

Ingredients:

- 3 cups spaghetti, cooked, broken in half
- 2 cups Pepperoni, sliced
- 6 eggs
- 4 cups ricotta
- 1 cup Parmesan cheese
- Salt and Pepper

Preparation:

Mix eggs with ricotta and parmesan cheese and season mixture with salt and pepper.

Fold ricotta mixture into pasta.

Divide pasta and sauce among mason jars and bake at 350F for 30 minutes.

Cool jars completely before serving.

## *Brown Rice and Veggie Jar*

Ingredients:

1 cup brown rice, cooked

½ cup mixed salad greens

1 small red onion, sliced thinly

½ small red bell pepper, chopped

½ small yellow bell pepper, chopped

1 teaspoon olive oil

2 teaspoons apple cider vinegar

Salt and pepper


Preparation:

Whisk together olive oil, apple cider vinegar and season with salt and pepper to taste.

Layer ingredients in jar following this order: dressing, bell peppers, brown rice and mixed salad greens.

Chill for a couple of hours before serving.

## *Baked Frittata*

Ingredients:

- 7 large eggs
- 4 pieces of sausage
- 2 cups crème fraîche
- 1 small red bell pepper, chopped
- ½ bunch of kale, chopped
- Salt

Preparation:

Preheat your oven to 400F.

Cook the sausage in a pan until cooked through.

Add the red bell pepper and kale and cook.

Whisk together eggs and crème fraiche in a large bowl.

Divide the meat and vegetable mixture between 6 wide mouth mason jars.

Top the jars off with egg mixture, leaving an inch headspace.

Bake until set and golden on top.

## *Curry Rice and Veggies*

Ingredients

- ½ cup cooked rice
- 2 tablespoon Tikka Masala
- 2 tablespoon cream
- ½ cup red bell pepper, diced
- ½ cup zucchini, diced
- 1 cup arugula

Preparation:

Combine rice, with the tikka masala paste and cream.

Add to the bottom of the jar.

Layer the different vegetables.

Seal the jar and refrigerate for future consumption.

# Chapter 4 - Dinner Jar Recipes

### *Barbecue Jars*

Ingredients:

- 2 cups baked beans, warm
- ½ cup store bought coleslaw, brought down to room temperature
- ¼ store bought barbecue pork, shredded
- 1 cup barbecue sauce

Preparation:

Put a thick layer of beans in jar.

Add a layer of coleslaw.

Top with a layer of shredded pork and 1 to tablespoon of your favorite barbecue sauce.


### *Mac and cheese*

Ingredients:

- 2 cups macaroni, cooked al dente
- 2 tablespoon heavy cream
- 1 tablespoon cream cheese, broken into small pieces
- 1 teaspoon spicy mustard
- 1 teaspoon of water
- 1/4 cup cheddar
- Salt and pepper

Preparation:

Combine cream, mustard, water and macaroni pasta. Put in the jar.

Mix cream cheese and cheddar cheese. Top pasta with the cheese sauce.

Season with salt and pepper before putting on the lid.

Store in the refrigerator

## *Shepherd's Pie*

Ingredients:

- 1 pound lean ground beef, cooked and seasoned according to taste.
- 1 tablespoon tomato sauce
- 6 cups mashed potatoes
- 1/2 cup freshly grated Parmesan
- 1/2 cup freshly grated sharp cheddar cheese

Preparation:

Preheat oven at 350F.

Mix cooked ground beef and tomato paste.

Put a layer of meat into jar.

Add a layer of cheeses and top it off with mashed potatoes.

Bake until top is golden.

Cool first before serving.

## *Pizza Jar*

Ingredients:

- 3 cups store bought pizza dough
- 1 cup tomato sauce
- 2 tablespoon dried basil
- 1 cup ground beef, cooked

- 1 medium size green bell pepper, chopped
- 1 medium size onion, sliced
- 1 cup mozzarella cheese

Preparation:

Preheat oven at 400F.

Mix ground beef, dried basil and tomato sauce. Put a layer of meat mixture in jar.

Add a layer of bell peppers, onion, and cheese.

Top with a layer of dough.

Bake until dough is brown and crispy.

Cool jars before serving.

## *Chicken Pot Pie*

- 1 can cream of chicken soup, heated through
- 2 chicken breasts, diced, cooked with soup
- 2 medium size potatoes, cooked diced
- 1 roll store bought pasty dough
- 1 tablespoon dried Italian herbs
- 1 tablespoon butter

Preparation:

Preheat oven at 400F

Put a layer of chicken and chicken soup in jar.

Put a layer of potatoes and a sprinkle of herbs.

Top with pastry dough and butter. Make sure to cut out vents on the dough.

Bake until dough is crisp.

Cool before serving.

# Chapter 5 - Snack Jar Recipes

### *Lazy Lemon Cheesecake*

Ingredients:

- 1 block cream cheese
- 1/2 cup milk
- 1 tub Cool Whip
- 1 package Jell-o Vanilla Pudding
- 1 cup lemon curd
- 1 pack graham crackers, crushed
- 1/3 cup butter, melted
- 2 tablespoons white sugar

Preparation:

Combine cream cheese, milk, cool whip, and vanilla pudding in a bowl.

Mix crushed grahams with butter and sugar.

Layer crust, cream, and lemon curd in jar in that order.

Top off with crushed grahams and chill in refrigerator for a couple of hours before serving.

### *Berries and Cream*

Ingredients:

- 1 container low-fat vanilla yogurt
- 1 container cool whip topping
- 3 cups fresh blueberries
- 4 cups strawberries, sliced
- 1/2 tsp. vanilla essence

Preparation:

Mix yogurt and vanilla essence and fold into cool whip topping.

Alternately layer cream, strawberry, and blueberry layers until mason jar is filled.

Chill for at least an hour before serving.

## *Peaches and Cream*

Ingredients:

- 1 Peach, diced
- ¼ cup granola
- ½ cup Cream
- Honey

Preparation:

Layer granola, cream, and diced peaches in a jar.

Drizzle honey on top.

Eat chilled.

## *Strawberry Dream*

Ingredients:

- Fresh Strawberries
- ¼ cup Granola
- ½ cup Greek yogurt with a drop of vanilla essence
- White Chocolate Shavings

Preparation:

Layer Granola, strawberries and yogurt in a mason jar.

Top with white chocolate shavings before chilling.

Add a dash of warm milk before serving.

## *Mango Surprise*

Ingredients:

- 1/4 cup granola
- 1/2 cup yogurt
- 1/4 cup mango, cubed
- 1 tablespoon flax seeds

Preparation:

In a bowl, mix yogurt and flax seeds together.

Layer granola, yogurt mixture and cubed mango in a mason jar.

Top with more mango and granola.

Chill for a couple of hours before serving.

## *Monkey Bread*

Ingredients:

- 10 pcs. biscuits, cut into quarters
- 1/2 cup dark brown sugar
- 1/2 cup sugar
- 1 teaspoon ground cinnamon

Preparation:

Preheat oven to 350 degrees.

Mix sugar and cinnamon. Add biscuit pieces and toss to coat in sugar mixture.

Place biscuit pieces into jars. Fill jars ¾ of the way and add more of the sugar mixture as you go along.

Bake jars for 15 minutes or until the bread has become bubbly and caramelized.

Make sure jars are cooled before serving.


## *Creamy Smoothie*

Ingredients:

- 1 cup coconut milk, almond or vanilla flavored
- 1 teaspoon vanilla essence
- 2 oranges, peeled, pitted, and cut into wedges
- 1 tablespoon coconut oil
- Ice

Preparation:

Add orange pieces, coconut milk, vanilla essence, and ice to blender.

Blend until smooth.

Add coconut oil and blend for a couple of seconds.

Pour into jars and serve. Chill in freezer for future consumption.


## *Cherry Nut Smoothie*

Ingredients:

- 1 cup coconut milk, almond flavour
- 1 tablespoon coconut oil
- 1 cup cherries, frozen
- ½ teaspoon almond extract
- 2 tablespoon honey
- 1 teaspoon cinnamon
- 3 tablespoons raw almonds, crushed

Preparation:

Add milk, almond extract, honey, raw almonds and frozen cherries in blender and blend until smooth.

Add coconut oil while blender is working.

Pour smoothie into jar and sprinkle cinnamon on top before serving.

## *Jolly St. Nick Smoothie*

Ingredients:

- 3 cups milk
- 1 frozen banana, cut into 4 parts
- 1 cup vanilla ice cream
- ½ teaspoon almond extract
- 2 dates, pitted, chopped
- ½ teaspoon nutmeg
- ½ cinnamon
- Candy cane

Preparation:

Add all ingredients in blender and run until you get a smooth consistency.

Pour into jar and garnish with a candy cane before serving.

# Chapter 6 - Dessert Jar Recipes

## *Vanilla Honey Panna cotta*

Ingredients

- 2 cups heavy cream
- ½ cup milk
- ½ cup sugar
- 3 sheets gelatin
- 1 teaspoon vanilla essence
- ¼ cup honey

Preparation:

Heat heavy cream, milk, sugar and vanilla bean in a pot and bring to a simmer.

Soak gelatin sheets in ice water for 5 minutes. Add gelatin to the hot cream and whisk. Allow to cool.

Spoon honey into the jars and chill in the freezer to set.

Pour the panna cotta on top of the honey and refrigerate for at least 2 hours before serving.

## *Butterscotch creme*

Ingredients:

- 1 1/2 cups heavy cream
- 6 tablespoons water
- 4 large egg yolks
- 1/2 teaspoon vanilla essence
- 6 tablespoons brown sugar
- 5 tablespoon high grade sugar
- 3 tablespoon unsalted butter, melted
- 1/4 teaspoon salt

Preparation:

Preheat oven to 300°F.

Bring cream, brown sugar, and salt just to a simmer. Stir occasionally to melt sugar completely.

Mix syrup and butter and fold into cream mixture.

Whisk together egg yolk and vanilla. Add to hot cream and whisk constantly.

Pour custard into jars and bake in oven in a hot water bath until it sets.

Make sure jars have cooled completely before serving.


## **Sinful Chocolate Pudding**

Ingredients:

- 4 large egg yolks
- 1¾ cups heavy cream
- ½ cup white sugar
- 1½ cups Guinness Stout, room temperature
- 2 cups high-quality dark chocolate, finely chopped

Preparation:

Whisk together egg yolks and sugar.

 Add guiness and cream to saucepan and whisk to combine. Bring to a boil.

Add chocolate and whisk until mixture is smooth.

Add egg mixture slowly. Make sure to whisk constantly to avoid curdling.

Bring back to heat and cook for 3 minutes.

Once the mixture thickens, pour into jars and refrigerate.

Chill overnight before serving.

## *Cherry Treat*

Ingredients:

- 3 cups cherry pie filling
- 1/2 cup rolled oats
- 1/2 cup all-purpose flour
- 1/4 cup butter, melted
- 1/3 cup packed light brown sugar

Preparation:

Preheat oven to 350F.

Add layer of cherry pie filling in jar.

Combine oats, flour, brown sugar and butter and mix.

Add crumble in jar.

Bake 20-25 minutes.

Serve warm. Perfect with a side of vanilla ice cream.

## *Chocolate Delight*

Ingredients:

- 1/4 cup cornstarch
- 1 cup sugar
- 1/2 cup baking cocoa
- 4 cups milk, warm
- 2 tablespoons butter
- 1/2 teaspoon salt
- 2 teaspoons vanilla extract

Preparation:

Combine cornstarch, sugar, cocoa and salt in a saucepan.

Whisk warm milk into the dry ingredients and bring to a boil.

Simmer for a couple of minutes, making sure that you stir frequently.

Stir in vanilla and butter and set aside.

Once the pudding is in room temperature, transfer to mason jar.

Chill pudding in refrigerator until it sets.

## Christmas Pies

Ingredients:

1½ cup oreo cookies, without the cream center, crushed

3 cups mini marshmallows, white

1 ½ cup cream, whipped

¼ cup crème de menthe

½ cup milk

1 cup dark chocolate shavings

Preparation:

Melt marshmallow and milk in a saucepan over low heat. Stir occasionally and wait for the mixture to thicken.

Add crème de menthe to the mixture. Set aside and allow to set.

Fold whipped cream into the mint mixture.

Create a crust in the jar, making sure to pack it down.

Add cream mixture on top of the crust.

Top with chocolate shavings.

Chill in refrigerator for at least 2 hours before serving.

## *Tropical cake*

Ingredients:

- 1 1/3 cup flour
- 1/2 teaspoon baking powder
- 1 egg, beaten
- 1 cup white sugar
- 1/2 teaspoon salt
- ½ cup butter
- 1 cup brown sugar
- 3/4 cup heavy cream
- 1/4 cup butter, melted
- 6 slices pineapple
- 6 maraschino cherries without stems
- 2 teaspoons of vanilla extract

Preparation:

Preheat oven to 350F.

Combine flour, baking powder, sugar, and salt in a large mixing bowl.

Add butter, vanilla, egg, and cream. Mix until you get a smooth cake batter.

Add melted butter and tablespoon of brown sugar into the jar and place in the oven to caramelize.

Add a pineapple ring and a cherry to the bottom of the jar before pouring cake batter. Allow at least 1 inch space from the top of the jar.

Bake until the top of cake is browned slightly.

Cool jar completely before serving.

## *Peach Cobbler*

Ingredients:

- 3 cups peach pie filling
- 1/4 cup butter, melted
- 1/2 cup bisquick mix
- 1/2 cup sugar
- pinch salt
- 1/2 cup milk

Preparation:

Preheat oven to 375F.

Combine bisquick mix, sugar, milk, and salt. Add melted butter and stir until you get a smooth batter.

Pour peach filling in jar 1/3 of the way.

Top filling with 2-3 tablespoons of batter.

Bake until the top becomes golden.

Cool jars before serving.

# Chapter 7 - Salad Jar Recipes

## *Grilled Chicken Salad*

Ingredients:

- 1 cup roasted chicken, cubed
- 1 cup lettuce, chopped
- 1 medium sized tomato, chopped
- 1 small green pepper, chopped
- 4 button mushrooms, thinly sliced
- 2/3 cup extra-virgin olive oil
- 1 tablespoon balsamic vinegar
- 1/4 cup orange juice
- 1 tablespoon dijon mustard
- Salt and pepper

Preparation:

Whisk extra-virgin olive oil, orange juice, balsamic vinegar and mustard together.

Layer dressing with chicken, lettuce, tomato, pepper, and mushroom.

Top with leaf lettuce.

Serve chilled.

## *Classic Mediterranean Salad*

Ingredients:

- 4 large tomatoes, chopped
- 2 medium size cucumber, chopped
- 2 cups Kalamata olives
- 1 medium size yellow pepper, thinly sliced
- 1 medium size red bell pepper, thinly sliced
- 1 small red onion, chopped

- 2 cups feta cheese, crumbled
- 1/3 cup Greek-inspired dressing

Preparation:

Add dressing to jar.

Layer cheese, onion, peppers, olives, cucumber, then lastly, tomatoes.

Chill at least 15 minutes before serving.

Shake to coat veggies with dressing before eating.

## *Italian Pasta Salad*

Ingredients:

- 2 cups grape tomatoes
- 2 cups fresh mozzarella
- 2 cups whole grain pasta, cooked
- 2 cups baby spinach
- 1 cup balsamic vinegar dressing

Preparation:

Layer ingredients in jars in this order: dressing, tomatoes, mozzarella, pasta, and lastly spinach.

Chill for at least 30 minutes before serving.

Shake jar to coat dressing.

## *Carribean Bean Salad*

Ingredients:

- 2 ripe avocados, peeled and cubed
- 1 can black beans, drained

- 1 1/2 cups quinoa, cooked
- 4 cups of spinach
- 2 ripe mangoes, cubed
- 1 tablespoon fresh lime juice
- 1 tsp apple cider vinegar
- 1/2 teaspoon honey
- 3 tablespoon extra virgin olive oil
- Salt

Preparation:

Gently toss avocado, mango and lime juice in a large bowl.

Whisk together apple cider vinegar, salt, honey and olive oil in a smaller bowl.

Following this order, layer dressing, black bean, quinoa, avocado and mango mixture, and spinach in jar.

## *Chicken Taco Salad*

Ingredients:

- 2 chicken breasts, grilled, shredded
- 1 cup canned corn
- 1 cup canned black beans
- 1 cup tomatoes, diced
- 1 cup lettuce, chopped
- 1 whole avocado, peeled and cubed
- 1/4 cup greek yogurt
- ¼ cup feta cheese, crumbled
- Juice of 1 whole lime
- 1/4 teaspoon cumin
- 1/4 cup water
- Salt

Preparation:

Make dressing by mixing together greek yogurt, feta cheese, lime juice, avocado, and water in a food processor. Puree until mixture is smooth. Season with salt to taste.

Layer ingredients in jar. Start off with dressing, then corn, black beans, tomatoes, chicken and lastly lettuce.

Keep in the refrigerator until ready to eat.

## Sardine Salad Jar

Ingredients:

- 1 can sardines, drained
- 4 grape tomatoes, chopped
- ¼ cup kale, chopped
- 1 cup mixed salad greens
- 1 teaspoon balsamic vinegar
- 2 teaspoons freshly squeezed orange juice
- 1 teaspoon lemon juice
- 1 tsp finely chopped fresh dill
- Salt and pepper

Preparation:

Whisk together balsamic vinegar, orange juice, lemon juice and season with salt and pepper to taste.

Layer ingredients in jar following this order: dressing, kale, sardines, watercress, tomatoes and salad greens.

Chill for a couple of hours before serving.

## Chicken Potato Salad

Ingredients:

- 5 cups potatoes, peeled, boiled, diced
- 1 large carrot, peeled, boiled, diced
- 1/2 cup celery, finely chopped

- 2 slices chicken fillet, grilled, diced
- 8 tablespoons mayonnaise
- 1 cup pineapple, diced
- Salt and pepper

Directions:

Layer potatoes, carrot, celery, pineapple, chicken fillet in a mason jar.

Top with mayonnaise and season with salt and pepper to taste.

Put the lid on and refrigerate for future consumption.

## **Chicken Macaroni Salad**

Ingredients:

- 2 cups elbow macaroni, cooked al dente
- 1 cup chicken, cooked, cubed
- ½ cup mayonnaise
- ½ cup ranch dressing
- 1 teaspoon mustard
- 1 tablespoon sugar
- 1 tablespoon apple cider vinegar
- 1 small red onion, chopped
- ½ cup canned corn
- 1 smal red bell pepper, chopped
- 1 stick celery, chopped
- 1 large carrot, chopped
- 1 teaspoon dried Italian seasoning
- Salt and pepper
- Preparation:

In a large bowl, mix all ingredients together.

Season with salt and pepper to taste.

Transfer salad to jar and refrigerate for a couple of hours, allowing the flavors to meld.

# Chapter 8 - Using Mason Jar Meals To Lose Weight

One of the great things about mason jar meals is that once you get into it, you'll find it easier to lose weight. How? Because it can help you with portion control.

I know a lot of people out there who struggle with overeating. With food servings getting bigger and bigger, it's become harder to take control over how much you eat. I know I was obsessed over it for a while because I wanted to lose the extra weight so bad. I could handle the food substitutions sure. I just couldn't handle the limited proportions.

By eating mason jar meals, it will be easier for you to train your body into thinking that 1 mason jar serving is enough as one meal. You'll be able to keep tabs of your portions without feeling deprived.

It may seem hard in the first few days, but once your body gets used to it, you'll feel like 1 jar is enough. It's all really about tricking your mind into it. And of course choosing fresh ingredients for your meals!

# Chapter 9 - Planning For Make Ahead Mason Jar Meals

Getting your fill of healthy meals doesn't have to be a challenge. Just follow these tips and you'll be set for the week!

- Look for fresh ingredients that are currently on sale at your local market and create recipes around them.

- Use coupons to save up on your food bill. Canned ingredients for example bulk up your mason jar meals, without the extra cost.

- Cook big batches of food and store half of them in jars for future meals. Don't forget to label your jars with the date they were made so you know when they should be consumed.

- Set aside some time over the weekend to cook up all your meals for the week. As long as you sterilize your jars before packing them with food, you won't have to worry about spoilage.

- Soups are great to make ahead because storing them in the refrigerator gives them more time for their flavors to blend.

# Chapter 10 - Storage Tips And Foods To Avoid When Making Mason Jar Meals

Although mason jars help food keep longer, you need to practice some precautions to ensure that you get fresh meals every time. Here are some helpful hints to keep in mind when making your mason jar meals.

- Assemble your salads properly. As a rule of thumb, dressing goes in first, next the sturdier ingredients, then the flimsier ones. This way, you can get avoid getting soggy greens next time you open up a jar salad.

- Always start off with pristine jars. Clean your jars and take time to sterilize them properly before your pack in your meals.

- Mason jars can withstand extreme temperatures, just not right after each other. Always allow jars with hot food to cool before storing in the refrigerator.

- Keep your cooking area clean at all times. Don't let food touch areas where bacteria can breed.

- Leave at least ½ inch of space at the top of the jar. Don't fill them up to the brim if you want to be able to seal them with a lid properly.

- Store food in jars in the refrigerator if you're not going to eat them.

- Once you open a jar, make sure that you consume the contents within 3 hours.

# Conclusion

Thank you again for purchasing this book on Delicious Meals in Mason Jars!

I am extremely excited to pass this information along to you, and I am so happy that you now have a better idea on how you can make the most out of make ahead meals.

I hope this book was able to help you understand just how convenient it is to make jar meals and how you can start creating your very own recipes.

What's the next step? Get started on these make ahead meals of course! With this guide in hand, you'll be on your way to a healthier and happier lifestyle.

But please don't be someone who just reads this information and doesn't apply it, the strategies in this book will only benefit you if you use them!

If you know of anyone else that could benefit from the information presented here please inform them of this book.

Finally, if you enjoyed this book and feel it has added value to your life in any way, please take the time to share your thoughts and post a review on Amazon. It'd be greatly appreciated!

Thank you and good luck!

# Preview Of:

# *Ultimate DIY Household Hacks Guide!*

# DIY Household Hacks

*Save Time, Money And Effort, Increase Productivity And Get Stuff Done With 120 Proven And Smart Household Hacks to Make Life Easier!*

# Introduction

I want to thank you and congratulate you for purchasing the book, *"DIY Household Hacks"*.

This "DIY Household Hacks" book contains proven steps and strategies on how to deal with common problems around the house.

The problems these hacks are trying to solve are encountered by everybody. These life hacks were thought of by everyday people. They have no special characteristics or skills other than their ingenuity. This means that you or anybody else living with you will be able to do these life hacks too. You will be able do some of them immediately after you read them. Some of them though, require a bit of practice to perfect.

Many people look up life hacks in the internet and are amused by them. They even share the website with these hacks on their social media accounts. However, these hacks are worthless if you don't use them one by one in your own household.

Thanks again for purchasing this book, I hope you enjoy it!

# Chapter 1: All About Life Hacks

Your home doesn't have to be messy or out of control. With the right knowledge and materials, you will be able to take control of all the areas around the house.

All the commercial household products you see in the television may make you feel that you always need to make a purchase to solve a household problem. This book will show you simple shortcuts to common household problems that you may be facing right now.

This book contains 120 of the most useful life hacks that you can apply in your own household.

Truth about Life hacks

In this book, the word "hack" refers to creative, easy and clever solutions to common problems; solutions anyone can use. They do not require any special equipment or devices, and the materials used are usually already in your own home.

Aside from the instructions suggested by this book, you should also think of how you can improve these hacks to make them fit your own situation. Not all of the hacks discussed in this book will help make your life better. However, reading about how other people solved common problems may give you ideas on how you can solve yours. All you have to do is to make use of the available materials around you creatively.

For your convenience, the household life hacks in this book are arranged according to their advantages. The life hacks that will help you save time, money and effort will be together in one chapter. The ones that aim to make you more productive at home will also be grouped together. The book is designed this way to make sure that you will easily find the life hacks that you want when you most need them.

# Thanks for Previewing My Exciting Book Entitled:

# "DIY Household Hacks: Ultimate DIY Household Hacks Guide! Save Time, Money And Effort, Increase Productivity And Get Stuff Done With 120 Proven And Smart Household Hacks to Make Life Easier!"

To purchase this book, simply go to the Amazon Kindle store and simply search:

"DIY HOUSEHOLD HACKS"

Then just scroll down until you see my book. You will know it is mine because you will see my name "Sarah Brooks" underneath the title.

Alternatively, you can visit my author page on Amazon to see this book and other work I have done. Thanks so much, and please don't forget your free bonuses

**DON'T LEAVE YET! - CHECK OUT YOUR FREE BONUSES BELOW!**

# Free Bonus Offer: Get Free Access To The www.LuxyLifeNaturals.com VIP Newsletter!

Once you enter your email address you will immediately get free access to this awesome newsletter!

But wait, right now if you join now for free you will also get free access to the "Anti-Aging Made Easy" free EBook!

To claim both your FREE VIP NEWSLETTER MEMBERSHIP and your FREE BONUS Ebook on ANTI-AGING MADE EASY!

Just Go To:

www.LuxyLifeNaturals.com

CPSIA information can be obtained at www.ICGtesting.com
Printed in the USA
LVOW10s1937230915

455415LV00027B/1603/P

9 781514 251393